The Poetic Verse (My Book of Rhymes)

Poetry Blog: www.amazulugaming.com
Instagram: Onepoeticgamer
Twitch: www.twitch.tv/onepoeticgamer

ISBN 979-8-9857102-0-5

Published by
AmaZulu Gaming, LLC

Cover Art work done by Billy Williams, Jr. and David Delgado

Final Edition
Printed in the United States of America

Table of Contents

Word on Wednesday

Thoughtful Thursday

Freestyle Friday

Preface

It has been an interesting journey watching my rhyme technique go from traditional rhyming poetry to my unorthodox rhyming style. I have been heavily influenced by hip-hop artist in creating my rhymes and I am thankful for having that music genre and culture in my life. I also want to give myself a shoutout for not forcing myself to create rhyming (or any form of poetry for that matter) in a way that someone else thought it should be. So, if you're an aspiring writer reading this, remember, "do you" and be unapologetic about it.

In this book, you will find a collection of rhyming poetry that I have written that spans from the early 2000's up to now. I hope you can enjoy reading my work and seeing how it developed throughout the years.

Word on Wednesday

Word On Wednesday
-whatever-

I got two options
-live or die-
so during this grind
I find I'll make the choice of a lifetime
where rubber hits the road and I pass go
forget the 200 dollars
as it wouldn't make it 3 weeks with gas prices
so I have to make something happen
whether it's peaceful or chaotic
ironic how this tonic keeps changing
keeps rearranging the situation
for me to one up my faith
laced with different aspects of hate
and what little sanity I do hold
I done did me one greater than Atlas
maxed this
weight, as I'm holding heaven on my shoulders
because it's easier than holding down hell
and if you couldn't tell
I'm on my P's and Q's
dotted my i's and j's
gone from A to Z
-twice-
I should be wearing the gold around my neck
but this ain't for competition

not for honorable mention
man…woman I do this cause my soul is on ice
be so cool with it
I blow out frost on open mics
during poetry night
while sitting outside in the summer time
getting mosquito bites
I'm half the hype your momma was
when yo daddy was her boyfriend
I'm not listening, I'm paying attention
none of this stuff is for free
it's costing me
just for some other man to sit on his ass in jail
so when I stick you up during the Good Times
don't say I'm unethical
just know I did it before someone else did
before someone even hungrier than me
went bananas and coo-coo at the same time
and figure they'd go gorilla for some coco puffs
I popped the clutch, my collar and bottles
all at the same time
just to prove I can do rap videos
while riding a 10 speed
there's something in me
and I know you don't want it
but you just gotta have it
gotta have some B's and Dots
mix it up with the Motts
and you now got a name brand applesauce
being promoted by a poet
I'm so loaded

you didn't know shit got stacked this high
and at 5'5"
I'm five times the dodo then you'll ever be
and that's not even braggin'
that's just my swag dripping with my afro
and I got yo
whatever right here
so let's go bowling
or make like a squirrel
running rampant on the street
with cars going both ways
looking crazy
like this poetic verse I'm kicking
got tired of pushing it
doing just what you through I shouldn't
and then making the best of it
and the best of this is yet to come
so keep your ears tuned, eyes open
and pencil ready
cause my part to this poem is now done.

Warm Up

I dream lavish
materialized into reality
so final fantasies can vanish
unloaded karmic baggage
need me a Latina chick
or one that's mixed
that can talk dirty to me in Spanish
love scenes, she and he
listening to H.E.R. sing Damage
soul flow, inner g
so we not limited to marriage
reflection eternal, unlearned societal habits
unlocked the chains to the game
and they will wonder how we manage
hands on but the inability to grab it
'94 warning, ring alarming
shoot the shot then take a stab at it
put out the APB, move ea-sy
on screen, crazy 4 wheeling
she rides, I drive, we coast on ATVs
please, I have the means or so it seems
to push the gas to move fast
you want the smoke, see these infrared beams
lean forward at the tape to win the race
I guess I anchor leg the team
despite war type tactics
I come in peace, love in my nature
let's go green…

Word Trade

I'm the poet working in produce
bagging your groceries
or serving sides with teas
and no one's noticing
my flow or art with these
other poet MCs, your local associate asking
did you find everything you're looking for
only to be ignored
watch you walk out the door
as my tour of duty is a gauntlet of job searches
where I get paid by the hour
at sold out venues that hold power
buy the girl I like flowers
only to be showered by rain
for five minutes of fame, damn shame
I've spent my sense
for crumbs and cents
convinced since my product
conducts heat but stays stuck
at the same warehouse I work at
that, or which, way I choose to move
from bottom to news, at the top
locs me in like hair from my crown
waves sound as if they'll crash
but I'll last with this inner push
to bring these words to past
with love, puff puff
catch this pass.

Poetic, I Said It

I transmuted my energy
to make this poetry
my poetic Kungfu
what I use to
bring thoughts to you
is the muse
that fuses the power like glue
to spirit, hope you hear it
before you feel it
that requires processing
before you cheer it
no need to A list
cause B Dots passes societal shifts
quick whiffs of the lyrical gift
has you at this
point, yet I'm writing with dull pencils
writing quintessential
what style is that you ask
and I laugh,
limitless but held with the task
of being remembered as
AmaZulu.

My Card (Unfinished)

My card
you pull it
and I check in like work time
cause on blue lines
I commit crimes
it's go time
like sunshine off recline
I drop dimes
2 times 5
got 4 eyes
still a fly guy
rocking bow ties
slinging bean pies
cause I don't try
I just get mine
since '8-9
when I was nay high
use to co-sign
on my first rhymes
use to be shy
use to be I
use to see my
use as knee high
but I grew sly
as I provide
what'cha need
now my roots tied
on the up rise
or the Upside

unless you drive by
then I nosedive
take a mean slide
to the inside
watch the boy glide
like my hang time
check the skyline
if it's light, I prefer lime
in the meantime
out to get mine
using my mind
no need to ask why
I bet I won't cry
and I don't lie
well, maybe sometime…

Poetic Flows

Spend half the day sleep
just so I can apply the phrase
-stay woke-
broke pockets equates to broke asses
so here's to me poking my nose
in big businesses in order to get the cash
last time I moved this fast
she was yelling for daddy
and proceeded to call me papi
if only I can stop me
then obviously this monopoly
and the only way you cop me
is to move one step past Marvin Garden
I would beg your pardon
but beggars can't be choosers
and my black credit card came in
we not the same and
I threw that credit card shit out the window
since my invitation to the group
comes from my Brown skin
I think of when it was a dream to be wealthy
but since then, my riches come from being healthy
move with stealth see, actually
you can't, I won't, they don't
fuck nots, they don't believe in me
and that includes family that's not focusing
you should be noticing by now
why it's better for me to sleep
cause when awake,
the earth quakes, skies levitate

and I drink milk shakes
for the shits and giggles
give me a bit of wiggle room
and I'll get out of a pickle
it can be all so simple
cause like Wu-Tang
I'm forever, no matter the weather
or whether or not you're ready
pop the confetti
cause when I come through, I'm rock steady.

affinity

I'm outta focus
and I notice
listening to your voice
got me in between comatose and
what's this, bliss
want me to tell you something
can't figure it out
we speak the same language
think less, feel more
intuitive clout
jumping out the box for it
nothing to fix
unless, it's
this separation that has our physical split
footed in grass patches with
my ear to the wind, soul lit
vibrations sent to shower you
did you get
the message I'm massaging
into your essence
was hesitant
life lyrics may be
a bit much to introduce my presence
unless, it's
matching pulsations that's prevalent
in which case
mirror reflected
seems we're convalescent
until we remedy it with
affinity.

Keep it Fly

Instead of taking the personification of hero
I became super, went to one from zero
for real tho,
probably didn't even notice
I am 10 on the scale
up I'm bout to blow this
kiss, to the dime piece that casually just floated
by, like Jesus saying that's so liquid
on sandals that's aero coated
duly noted, then told this to my future
drank a Red Bull and it grew wings
so when I fly subsequently
you could say I speak prophetic things
I mean, I was bound to make it happen
clipped the chains, airfoil said strings
and by the time you understand what happened
I'll be healing in hot springs.

This is My Call Back

(Left a Message)

It's all peace
like naturally Shaunice
casually I speak
eyes open, here's a peek
a verse to make ya peep
this flow, I'm going deep
to see if it will reach
your heart and mind, I seep
into while reaching peaks
put songs on loop, repeat
til you can feel this beat
till knees are getting weak
until this one's complete
there's something that I seek
(pause)
underneath, I creep to meet
you find lyrics too sweet
(uhh)
adding heat, I sneak and leak
these words like tasty treats
and,
just know growth happens
if you let it, hear me clappin
for those milestones that you meetin'
in alignment has you tappin'
into places some can't see
but you are makin', facts, no cappin'
I salute you, aye' aye' captain

if you want, come give you dap and,
I slow it down
since there ain't no need to rush
sending you this candy crush
baby, this candy crush.

Verses from The Poetic One

Yeah…yeah
Yeah…yeah
Let's go…
It's like my dreams contemplate things
so I go back in time
it's like the sun on grand rising
not having a sky to shine
in, my friend, cause when, she sends
a heart, just might this be a sign
rewind these horses before the cart
and sit back to unwind

I said it's like my dreams contemplate things
so I go back in time
it's like the sun on grand rising
not having a sky to shine
in, my friend, cause when, she sends
a heart, just might this be a sign
rewind these horses before the cart
and sit back to unwind

I blend slow, dream of driving benzos
my ends low, so my beginnings can now
and then show
how high I spend those, I might go
where no man has been be-fo'
opposite of Lerenzo
hide she in he just so you won't know
oh please, just breathe, gold keys

pop these, car-le tows thoughts that won't stop
when the wind blows
gas up and set fire so I'm set to explode
so beautiful, soap opera, guess I should be that bold
enough to touch her heart like
no one else so when told
this story is never ending,
the nothing is now something
so hot and yet so cold
I know…yeah, I know…

It's like my dreams contemplate things
so I go back in time
it's like the sun on grand rising
not having a sky to shine
in, my friend, cause when, she sends
a heart, just might this be a sign
rewind these horses before the cart
and sit back to unwind

I wonder when you seek the truth
is love to hard to find
when landing on the moon,
do you realize it doesn't shine
in, my friend, cause when, she sends
a heart, should I take this as a sign
blind in the year 20/20
but see it all with the eye in my mind.

I sit, I think, meditate and wait with much debate
with higher self in my space

where you can find me safe
to face reality of what is actually taking place
my haste to make it happen cause races to be raced
relocate this hate that chaffed like pain
when kicked below the waist
the taste of great-ness is all I want
so that's all I contemplate
rotate the stove to a high degree
this flow is good and baked
wake up in this mid of morning
cause Spirit knows no time, so late
is much like being overdue
high powers gon' beat the case
my fate the same as destiny
I choose dates to recalibrate
that makes earth shifts when I adjust
that happens when you pass the plate
can find O.P. in his element
and N.C. is the mind I state.

It's like my dreams contemplate things
so I go back in time
it's like the sun on grand rising
not having a sky to shine
in, my friend, cause when, she sends
a heart, just might this be a sign
rewind these horses before the cart
and sit back to unwind

I wonder when you seek the truth
is love to hard to find

when landing on the moon,
do you realize it doesn't shine
in, my friend, cause when, she sends
a heart, just might this be a sign
blind yet it's 2020
but see clearly in my mind.

Thoughtful Thursday

Free Flow on Thursday

Gonna type this on the fly
make you realize
I'm that guy
that don't see eye to eye
because I fly while you drive by
oh say, you see, oh my
as I live the by and by
I make words cry
I do, not try
since Yoda is my guided Jedi
so let me wave bye
when you say hi
opposites attract
like two weeks that get called bi.

The Breakdown

When it rains outside
I reflect from the look in your eyes
on what it means to me on the inside
see where I reside is beyond the skies
cosmic love that reaches where
you choose to hide
I'm sublime so confide through lines
sent in telekinetic forms that come
from your mind to mine's
21st century, but we can still dine
over plates and dates
romance that combines
lights from candles despite the soul shine
from where I am sitting
you look like perfection, aged like fine wines
time is finite, so find me aligned
like planets that circle a bright star
there's love, I'm thinking of, that you remind
me, can it be, I see 360 degrees
and you still snuck up from behind
as I'm inclined now to give pause
and unwind in the breakdown of universal design.

Let's Switch Positions

No one sees me sitting here
battling self, everything in me
saying protest, get the vest, prepare for death
and I can't stop these tears from rolling
holding on to my sanity by quietly whispering
to the Universe, destined to break the curse
I feel at my best and my worse
skydiving but head first
you thirst, and I have the knowledge to prepare
cause I use to not care
and I can feel it in the air
Spirit moves from over there
and get here next to me
dream this my destiny, at 21 bought kufis
at 42 my locs have grown past two feet
I wish this cop knew me
I wish those not African-American could truly
understand how it feels to want to go for a walk
but think twice cause this could be
the last time, not like this
I shouldn't have to take this toolie
shouldn't have to explain why some are unruly
justice, that's fooey, if only, here's to the
day when I was profiled racially and I was just 18
shit got me thinking, while you keep blinking,
let me shift thoughts, please listen
can't just say fuck the cops
cause I got family in those positions
look at the dilemmas I sit in

I just want to go outside
and not get shot with my hands raised
a knee on my throat, comply and still get tased
kicked in the rib cage
sucker punched and then pepper sprayed
6 feet, not trying to get laid
I'm questioned like the villain I've been made
blamed but wait, I did pay
this my house, how can they just invade
let me pass the ball, here you play
and that's how your silence feels
while you watch, my people get slayed.

Intentions Set, Let's Manifest

What's sweet is
you're reading this verse
and I'm lurking behind the scenes
within your soul
sipping on the bubbly
where you and me mash up buttons
on game night
streaming live for the limelight
and this just feels right
despite being left to our own devices
what's nice is
the attempt to synchronize our lives
through similar situations
different forms of meditation
in overdrive before overtime
in and out of line somehow combined
so let's find our way
midday classics are quite fantastic
I'm tasked with refocusing conscious thought
to allow pathways to be free for passes
that seek completion, yes indeed this
is the flow for manifesting
dream so big there's no room to fizz
out the promised blessing
came back to life to learn the lesson
in this form, through these means
and we've been waiting on this moment
these choices you and I have to make
for this to be great, this to be fate

in present days, ancient ways
help pave this path before it's too late
as I walk towards you, our force
with situations at hand
I extend my choice
to us that's checkmate
and maybe, just maybe
this time...we get it.

My Gamer Girl, Looking For
(Adventure Awaits)

I switched it up (yup)
started to Twitch just to mix it up
Mixer that's mastered game socially
but that's solo, how bout a duo to tip the cup
of tea, can it be
my gamer girl is looking for me
let me hook this one right
then Marvel that D follows C,
I'm a G that's OP
unorthodox when matched in the box
clocked on a time limit so we don't stop
atop the mountain in a battle royale
while listening to hip-hop,
circle forever shrinking, let's make this team work
what better way than a co-op
-eration, anticipating what we could be making
as adventure awaits, this is ground breaking
digging this foundation using my real time strategy
actually, wouldn't mind if the roles we
played in game was Japanese
meet up together to console on consoles
better yet let's make it Personal,
Computer love is happening
as I muse, you seem to use
different genres to digitally draw me to
(whew)
how do I choose
-I Know-

how about you come through, so we can do
some local game play for a game or two
my gamer girl, I clipper board
that's your cue
as paradise awaits, come game with me
in AmaZulu.

Crescent

Create - that's how we relate
feel that breeze
that's me touching your face
that liquid sound
I remembered to hydrate
as I drink from your pools
of thought,
I don't mind being thirsty
if you can fulfill
cause what I'm about to fill
you with, can't be found in a mil
maybe even a bill-ion
equal to nil, sun like heat
in moon lit eyes
not sure you realize
how this ties to past lives
wait, right, you read this in the cards
one night, foresight
what's next as we're here
gazing in the other's eyesight
might, I be loved when
she calls me beloved
or was it as it always has been
and should think nothing else of it
no need to covet, as this
passing of waves roll eloquently
and currently the ride is good enough
on Earth, it's heavenly.

Can We Talk

(Brown Eyed Girl)

I'm the type that likes
your smile that's bright
when your lip curls up
and pearly whites down bite
the type that sits at night
in candlelight
listening to Sade recite,
something like
Kiss of Life
right before my eyes close tight,
the type that might
go left just to treat you right
or smite the hate
so love can fight
for peace I sink my teeth in plight
just so you can taste the sweet in life
the type that hypes
the games we like
a war that crafts
or mobile device
that clash I tell
ya might as well
face me off in battle royale
set sail, wind trials we tail
I fell, from a height that's like
high as sun light
so come hold this kite which feels so lite
since I'm the type

that says things twice
cause when you nice
that's how you splice
catch that, pitch two
I'll serve on ice
that's one + one is One - unite
like black and white
yep, I'm the type
that freaks ya name in things I write
Sha-ski-a right
Miss John is quite
tasty, I mean, you seem polite
I scribed this using hematite
as I roll the dice
know I'm the type
that stands for truth
wait, hold up, sit tight
I like to forthright use a foresight
in the next line I type
(hard pause)
I want to know your soul
(tosses you the pen) - will you playwright?

Soul Lurking

What's underneath
the mask you keep
the one we see on IG
let me peep
what's it like when you're asleep
when you're free
living the dream
I bet that's a sight to see
the inner you
that just wants to be
incredibly, apparently
unless I erroneously
felt this pleasantry
of vibe you sent soulfully
soundlessly, created the
poetry you and now read currently
I'm hoping we or is it me
that wants or need
something I'm not mentioning
that only could be picked up spiritually
manifested through quantum chemistry
shit, maybe this went too deep
poetically I went beyond fleek
as I just wanted to get underneath
your mask, count your math
pick the path not many seek
combine my imagination secretly
commit mindful intimacy
infinitely, repeatedly
with you.

Let's Shift Higher

Let's turn from uncommon belief
to impossible relief
blink and it could be missed
that feeling to get to this
with, open doors that switched
from pure logic
to nostalgic,
upon release of preconceptions
learned lessons that helped when planning
this moment, unexpected
yet expected
"traditional" that's outdated
"normal" restrictions thoroughly contemplated
grateful for this patience
kept alive to make this statement
of how we can shift higher
work this like magnets
were we attract without force
of course, that's us in unity
if the choosing
is lead with love and not fear
no one will end up losing.

Bring Back What's Mine

Finding myself in tales
without fairy
is this a part of the score
tangled in webs weaved by many
situated somewhat like folklore
it's a bit more than a muse
something like bees to honey
knocking on wood so she opens up the door
figured if I'm the light in darkness
my shot is valid, quite valid
I could embrace her once more
believe it to my core
despite mind tricks made for survival
let me know if I should even explore
because if anything
you can put that on everything
not sure what would be in store
but the trust is a must
minus just lust
and it's time for an encore.

Signal

My poems now come forth as frequencies
so there's no need to get angry
if she or he doesn't get it,
I'll let this tone ring until it's received
it can be disappointing, humanly
so spiritually these flows keep rolling
off the top of my ambience
tip of the semblance
when reminiscent of archaic language
only an old soul will know
low and behold to those
not connected to woke me
I find it comforting to write this in my sleep
just so we can level and
I still attain my high in 5th dimension
sitting in water tubs to be
in balance with my element
then rain this ele-mental composition
upon you like wet kisses
or that same amount of bliss at climaxes
that you can't miss when going for it
out the blue, off the cuff, while in the rough
with the odds stacked against you,
so forgive me if I come across as
the under dog, read backwards
sun that shines so bright
they recognize my aftermath as shady
and maybe I'm full of myself

which I find better than being left on empty
similarly, to life lessons handed to me
so who are we fooling when doodling
and twiddling our thumbs
didn't succumb
to the karmic reverberating shock wave
my soul asked for
shadow imprinted on the ground
still looking for more
still watching my core implode
in order to coordinate the forthcoming chaos
forgotten in historic lore
so I implore, you to tune in
and tune out the white noise
when processing in on
this signal.

Freestyle Friday

Freestyle Friday - 12-5-08

I don't cook ice
I spit it,
so cold with this
got renamed B-Dot Frosty,
I'm the reason why they wearing Chinchillas
in the summer time
concrete, block head
screaming lyrics to the Charlie Brown theme song
cause-I-be-that
poe-t, named-B-Dot
dun-dun-dun-dun,
got Snoopy dancing on the punch line
don't box, unless it's shadows
which makes me my own worst enemy
beat myself into oblivion
so I can R.I.P. the open mic
can't write as fast as I think
so I forget 95% of me being nice
be too graphic at certain moments
so I draw novels with my words
I heard why the caged bird sings
and set-em loose with my free verse,
cause THIS - IS - POETRY
worldwide, outside the box
it's too crowded in my cubicle
brushing elbows with those opposed
to my theories
dialect my rhetoric - correct

to make sure that you can hear me
people use to fear B.
Dot your eyes before you cross t's
cause he's really unapologetic
if coming up against the
spoken word
they screaming my parables at night
cause I'M - A - PO - ETTTTT
OUT - OF - ORDEEERRRR
well...kinda...sort of
but, if you don't believe me
check the bottom of my sneeks
cause I'm kicking flavor in your ear
ya mouth piece
and your noggin',
bloggin' my thoughts daily
so I EXCEL my POWER to the POINT
where my WORDS have ACCESS
so my World Wide Web
is in the Palm of my hands
so let me help you be an Explorer
with my Navigator
rev up my Engine to Search this madness
gotten off task cause I'm at this High Speed
tight ropin' on this Cable
see I'm able to calculate the distance
between the poetic mortar
and my perceived target
-so-
ROUNDS OUT! ROUNDS OUT!
I'm trying to blow my thoughts into your existence
this is my Viva La Resistance
and I'm coming to a theater near you!

Playlisted

Free flow, free throw
faith grows, faith goes
if you say so
I know I go
high if you move low
fast paced but seem slow
what do I owe to show
that I propose
these thoughts you now hold
feels hot but served cold
and I believe you've been told
one way, long road
hard times paid tolls
so no trolls can demand those
riches, experienced
in life trials that paid me distant
visits with higher Spirit
not sure if you aren't awaken
that you'd get this.

Freed the Verse

Instead of 50 shades of grey
here's 50 shades of me
make light of shadowed situations
now you got 6 degrees separately
find the variables I'm tossing at you
and while you're focusing
on unidentified flying objects
moving backwards, liking to take
-a moment-
to you, you're not even noticing
I'm up to bat, the state I'm in
not really known for its swing
back and forth is this movement
listening to The Weekend sing
ping this memento to your vision board
sensors triggered from motioning
check the glove, you made a catch
all this work was for something
comforting, wait, comfortably
comfort you until it's reversibly
like uno except it's duos
that's our comfortability
really starting to wonder if it's too deep
dialectical material warped into a peep
seek that which you been searching for
here, why don't you take a peek
seep these words into your intangibles
the show must go on but I'll be here all week.

Negroes Need to Collaborate
(B-Dot's Verses)

Negroes need to collaborate
B-Dotta why won't you elaborate
I conversate, then congregate
these poetic skills that's kinda great
shout my shit, avoid the hate
shout you back, now let's debate
your flow is smooth and mine's got weight
put us together, let's get this cake
dollar signs evaporate
stacks pile up with Jackson's face
can't keep the pace, cause we erase
the competition and then replace
no I in me, we form a team
now we got even bigger dreams
it's not just quite just what it seems
watch ying and yang, when they do their thing
B-Dot, oh shit
Latee, ill spit
once
we
do
this
you
can't
stop
it
Latee, oh shit

B-Dot, ill spit
T
O
Y
ISH
2
0
1
6

I creep
into this one
slow, so you will know
just
who I say I be
speed this up cause I'm the OPG
watch dis boy quick load the shots
pop pop pop
and watch them drop
I foil the plot then keep it hot
so call the cops and give up the gwap
as I lead the flock in my polo socks
til I reach the tip at the mountain top
you can't hip if you ain't got no hop
no need to flip when shit just flopped
cause I tend to block
tie ya up in knots
give the kid his props
so forget me not
cause I got the mott's

I'm the one to watch
give electric shock
to anyone who's not
trying to see
this dope ass team
B-Dot, Bullock
O-M-G

Now now now
we settlin'
360 where we began
I got my bros, no need for friends
not in this shit just chasing ends
I'm setting trends
and blazing trails
you call this heaven
gonna give you hell
cause I'm pippin hot
and if you couldn't tell
you can catch my comet
and grab the tail
cause we bustin out
there's no need to bail
so follow me
as I set sail
on a trip that's going
around the world
calling man, woman
every boy and girl
take ya on a twirl
give it a swirl

hit the lottery
diamonds and pearls
get my Prince on
confuse the real world
make a come back
never unfurled
so as I uncurl
what'cha goin' see
is B, Latee as we hurl…

Illusionary

Pillow talk is like when Jesus walks
only this is intimate beyond
a word like expect
fuck flexing this mic
I flex my breath
in bars that's liquid
that's 6 shots on the bard
locked up these here lyrics
guess I spit behind bars
bar none, I'm the one
poetic I'm called
use to be them vs me
now it's me vs y'all
below average in height
but from their view I'm quite tall
cellular in the make up
move in wavelengths when hauled
installing my memories
that got stalled while in stalls
that's me writing poems
in books that got paused
lone wolf, feel these paws
since I'm out, fuck these laws
want to be, it's my cause
I like art, here's my draw
-ings, what I mean
I'm jumping like said beans
setting off, turned it on
cause I'm not what I seem.

Let's Get It (Feels Good)

I take words out the air
put them together
it's magic
call it spoken word
syllables kiss my lips
it's quite fantastic
ever everlasting
spells that I'm casting
get called love poems
I guess I'm a chick magnet
moving too fast
let me slow down my cast with
poetic feats, Uber eats
first date was great
she didn't even know I asked, it
was love at first sight
think I might, found my wife
she breathes life, I'm tapping
out, don't doubt
what the vibe's about
shout to the top of my lungs
water works, reversed droughts
make moves that end down south
mouth to mouth feels good
you know what I'm talking bout
tout, confidence
that can fill up the Earth
since birth knew my worth
got the gift, broke the curse

nurse smacked me on the butt
winked my eye, told her that works
I'm a flirt, between spurts
blurt lines out like
I like it when you twerk
slight smirk, if you scared
I might as well go first
ancestors talk to me above ground
so there's no need to talk to the dirt
lurk, between here but go there
when they said "Imma tell yo mamma"
I yelled out "I DON'T CARE"
yeah, this that feel good poetic flow
got it locked up like my hair
but you don't hear me tho.

It's Like That

I see ya face
the feelings new
-it's like that-
I watch the sky
turn green to blue
-it's like that-
I'm feeling good
because of you
-it's like that-
she likes my lips
now what it do
-it's like that-
they say we one
but it takes two
-it's like that-
I say right
then you say true
-it's like that-
our love a seed
look how it grew
-it's like that-
before the weeeee
there comes an ooooo
-it's like that-
her taste is sweet
she thought I knew
-it's like that-
I love her spirit
now that's my boo

-it's like that-
we drinking Tang
like it's the Wu
-it's like that-
a work of art
look what I drew
-it's like that-
if it fits
I got the shoe
-it's like that-
read her book
it's overdue
-it's like that-
I'll walk behind her
I like the view
-it's like that-
she feels my lyrics
I got a few
-it's like that-
I shoot my shot
a pew, pew
-it's like that-
my love a potion
I got the brew
-it's like that-
a night owl
she's asking who
-it's like that-
lone wolf
straight out the zoo
-it's like that-

let's switch it up
while this one's hot
-it's like that-
sending love
forget me not
-it's like that-
you got the time
I'd like to watch
-it's like that-
if this the climax
then what's the plot
-it's like that-
put the gloves on
B throwin' dots
-it's like that-
you got next
then what you got
-it's like that-
since this the end
I have to stop
-it's like that-

Love on Sight

After scoping the scene
I had the means to your location
and the situation just got real
by way of this dedication,
sending shots your way
that's going to enter your anatomy
the chest cavity
face full of jabs with these
dots making the blood pressure drop
heart stops, mind clocked
as these, butterflies moving at
speeds that seem super sonic
not quite bionic
more so iconic mixed in with this tonic
and I'm on it, quite ironic
when free no need to keep it in the closet
back to my target
bullseye, steady with the aim
adjust to the wind dynamics
my shot above average
we not playing no games
brain talking about grey matters
but your soul feeling the change
as I release this heat that seeks to peek
in places where your tears have leaked
through foreign tongues that we both speak
secrets we share and choose to keep
could be discrete but when you and I meet
a duel of sorts but what's been reached

is love on sight, that's souls at peak
level, what a taste so sweet
elite in that it's worth repeat
a treat to taste when souls reach peaks
let's greet each other beside the creek
it's my belief, I find relief
inside the peace in one so meek
so let's increase, our bond forthright
because this a love…
a love on sight.

Thoughts On Free

Coordinate chaos, moves precise
unorthodox poet, with words concise
turn left, just so
they field it right
day trip just so we can chill on the set at night
I got the low low price
with the lo lo dice
I'm on high, but got the low-key flight
Lauren Wood, yeah she LoLo nice
flows like Ayscue, yeah my man's Lo he tight
veins be blue blood through red meat
that's beef on sight
you only live once
déjà vu, part two
I guess I get to do this twice
third time be the charm
bracelets on the wrist will suffice
I like salt and some pepper
it doesn't matter if ya black or white
don't wish I may because I just might
show those that dark
makes light look bright
don't sweat the technique
exercise the mind when I write
this be my food for thought
poetically, respectfully
aight.

100
(Verse One)

Age makes no difference
and on these things we can relate
not under cover
so there's no need to paint your face
I took a sip
and now I want some more to taste
I'm out of order
so Poetic had to take his place
and hold this space
if you agree, let's make this move
I got the plans
so it's only right I make the rules
a law that's out
no more will I be paying dues
I found the rhythm
no need for me to keep the blues
I'm asking who
cause I don't know where this one goes
you are the factor
how is it still that no one knows
still room to grow
move to and fro
I got to show
go with the flow
from knees to toes
fucks with no hoes
say it ain't so
still love the dough

cause I'm not po'
the nose it knows
the winters cold
about to blow
you say fa sho'
and then I hit you with the whoa
(pause)
cause what are those
no need for oh
green light means go
so I cast slow
my magic dozed
you off to sleep and I'm like yo
no status quo
to undergo or reach plateaus
I mean, although
this amateur destroying pros
I wave goodbye
and say hello.

About The Author

Billy Williams, Jr. was born to write poetry. Poetically knows as B-Dot and OnePoeticGamer, the life as a poet all started because of a girl back in 7th grade. Seeing he had a gift with words, he began to use his energy to produce poetry that spoke to various genres.

Hailing from Raleigh, North Carolina, Billy is a poet, educator, coach, gamer, streamer and motivator. The Poetic Verse - My Book of Rhymes is Billy's sixth book of published poetry, with more poetry books to be released in the near future.

If you want to find out more information about Billy's upcoming books, you can contact him by way of e-mail at onepoeticgamer@amazulugaming.com or sending a message to him from the following website www.amazulugaming.com. If you wish to know more about his gaming/streaming life, check him at www.twitch.tv/onepoeticgamer.

Social Media Contacts

Poetry Blog: www.amazulugaming.com
Instagram: Onepoeticgamer
Twitch: www.twitch.tv/onepoeticgamer

AmaZulu Gaming, LLC

Poetry Books Written By One Poetic

Poetic Superhero

Everybody is looking for a hero. Poetic Superhero is here for you.

The I prElude I

In order to find we, HE must find himself before finding SHE.

His Emotions Released

This is written for Her…I'm glad I finally got Her attention.

School Dad

Poetry inspired by 16 years of working as an educator in elementary, middle and high school.

the Book of HER

33 poems for HER.

The Poetic Verse - My Book of Rhymes

When I feel the flow, I let go with words.

Excommunicated (A Bard's Tale) (7/11/22)

Exit wounds given by another can lead to one's salvation.

A Bit More Than a Muse (11/11/22)

When she's a bit more than friend but doesn't recognize it yet.

Leftover Love Poems (2023 Release)

Sometimes you'll get things humanely wrong just so your soul can get right.

HER - The Collection (Poetry Anthology) (Future Release)

Includes works from The I pr.E.lude I, His Emotions Released and the Book of HER.

Spoken Word By One Poetic

Blue Room Mix Tape (upcoming soon)